# MOVING FORWARD

## *Navigating Sibling Grief*

*written by* Lin Law

*In Memory of Jamehl & Sandra Law*

Publishing By: DemiCo National, LLC

www.DemiCoNational.com

# Dedications

*For My Brother, Jamehl Law*

This book, born of devastation and built on love, is dedicated to the one person who defined protection, presence, and possibility in my life: my brother, Jamehl Law.

They say that when you lose a sibling, you lose a witness to your life. For me, losing Jamehl was like losing the central foundation of my world. He was more than a witness; he was my constant guardian, the quiet hero who always looked out for me, no matter the situation. In every challenge I faced, in every moment of doubt, Jamehl was simply there—a steady, unshakeable presence that anchored my existence.

His absence, marked by the terrible, sudden silence of an unexpected loss, created a void that is impossible to measure. But in the year since, I have come to realize that the immense love he gave did not vanish. It is the fuel, the guiding light, and the inspiration behind every word you read here.

Jamehl, your spirit, your unwavering kindness, and your effortless way of making me feel safe live on. This is my attempt to take the extraordinary way you looked out for me in life and turn it into a guide to look out for others in their grief. I carry you forward.

### *And for My Sister, Sandra Law*

This book also carries the light of my beloved sister, Sandra Law. Sandra was the architect of my life, both as a child and as an adult. Older and wiser, she took care of me—a role that never diminished, only deepened with time. She wasn't just my sister; she was my absolute best friend, the keeper of our shared history, and the quiet coordinator of every precious memory.

Losing her to complications with lupus was a slow, agonizing preparation for an absence that still feels unreal. The constant vigilance and the long goodbye have been replaced by a gaping hole, especially during the holidays—those days we meticulously spent together—that now arrive with a silent, sharp emptiness. I miss her like crazy, in the way you miss your own breath. But Sandra, your love taught me the greatest lesson of all:Resilience.

The fierce, nurturing spirit you showed while facing your illness, and the dedication you poured into caring for me, cannot be wasted. I continue to go on, to show up, and to fight for my own forward movement, because the thought of you looking down and being sad that I stopped is a motivator more powerful than any grief. This book is a continuation of your care, Sandra. It is your hand in mine, guiding others through the darkest days.

Thank you for never letting me go.

Dedication To Mickey and Scottie, my brothers, my anchors, my heart's home— your love lights the darkest days, your laughter echoes in every memory, and your presence reminds me that family is forever.

To my parents, whose arms have always held me, whose wisdom and love have guided me, and whose hearts remind me that even in sorrow, love never fades. This book is for you, for the love that surrounds me, and for the bonds that endure beyond time.

Dedication To my beloved nieces, Laila and Brook, the shining lights of Jamehl's legacy, may you always carry his love, courage,

and spirit within you.

You are the living proof that love never ends, that even in loss, hope blooms, and that your father's strength, laughter, and heart will guide you every day.

May this book remind you that you are capable, resilient, and deeply loved. Your journey is your own, but you will always walk it with his love beside you, and with the unbreakable bond of family to lift you through life's storms.

*-Lin Law*

# A Personal Note from the Author

When we lose a sibling, it feels as though a part of our soul has been taken. Siblings are more than family—they are our first friends, our mirrors, our challengers, and our confidants. They share in our triumphs and failures, shape our understanding of the world, and leave imprints that last a lifetime.

In 2022, I lost my sister, Sandra Faye. She was my confidante, my companion in laughter and in life's challenges. Her absence left me unmoored, navigating grief that I had never anticipated. Just as I began to face that loss, in 2024, I lost my brother, Jamehl. The pain of losing him compounded the grief I was already carrying, leaving me in a space of profound sorrow and reflection.

Through these losses, I realized how uniquely challenging sibling grief can be. Unlike parents, partners, or children, siblings are often overlooked in conversations about mourning. Our grief is quiet, misunderstood, and sometimes dismissed, yet it is deep and enduring. I discovered that there are few guides to help surviving siblings navigate this journey with understanding, compassion, and practical support.

I wrote this book to fill that gap. It is born from love, loss, and the desire to honor Sandra Faye and Jamehl. It is also a companion for every sibling who has faced the silent, persistent ache of losing a brother or sister. Within these pages, you will find reflections on grief, coping strategies, ways to preserve memories, and guidance for rebuilding life while keeping your sibling's presence alive in your heart.

This book is not just about surviving grief—it is about living with it, honoring those we have lost, and finding meaning in a life forever touched by love. My hope is that it provides comfort, insight, and courage to all who are walking the difficult path of sibling loss. Because while grief may never fully disappear, love—and the bond we share with our siblings—endures.

# TABLE OF CONTENTS

# Introduction of Chapters

Sibling grief is one of the most profound yet often overlooked forms of bereavement. While the death of a parent or child is widely acknowledged as life-altering, the loss of a sibling is sometimes minimized or ignored by society—despite the fact that siblings are often individuals' first friends, first rivals, first playmates, and lifelong witnesses to their personal development.

This write-up explores sibling grief in depth: the emotional, psychological, spiritual, and family-system impacts; how grief differs across ages; and how siblings can be supported through healing.

## The Unique Bond Between Siblings

Siblings share a history that no one else can replicate. This bond can be:

- genetic/biological
- emotional
- environmental (shared home, culture, family traditions)
- experiential (growing up together)

Siblings often play multiple roles in one another's lives:

- best friends
- confidants

* rivals

* protectors

* witnesses to childhood

* co-survivors of family challenges

Because of this layered relationship, sibling grief can be incredibly deep and complex.

## Understanding Sibling Grief

Sibling grief refers to the emotional, mental, and behavioral responses experienced when a brother or sister dies. It can include:

* sadness

* anger or guilt

* confusion

* identity disturbance

* role displacement

* anxiety about future loss

Sibling grief is often called "disenfranchised grief," meaning society does not fully acknowledge its depth. Many people expect parents or spouses to be the "primary" mourners, unintentionally leaving surviving siblings unsupported.

Why sibling grief is often overlooked:

1.  People assume siblings "weren't as close."

2.  Parents' grief may overshadow the sibling's grief.

3.  Siblings may hide their feelings to avoid burdening the family.

4.  There may be pressure to "be strong."

# Types of Sibling Loss

Sibling loss varies depending on circumstances.

**Loss in Childhood**

A child loses a brother or sister to illness, accident, or sudden trauma. This can disrupt development and create fear of losing others.

**Loss in Adolescence**

A teenage sibling dies during a time when identity formation is crucial. Grief may interrupt social, academic, and emotional development.

## Loss in Adulthood

Losing a sibling as an adult can create a sense of losing one's personal history, family continuity, and emotional anchor.

## Loss of an Infant or Stillborn Sibling

Even if the sibling was not known personally, the grief can still be real—centered on the idea of what "should have been."

## Loss of a Step-sibling or Half-sibling

Relationships vary, but the grief can still be deep when emotional closeness exists.

## Loss to Suicide

This brings layers of confusion, guilt, and anger.

## Loss to Violence

This can create trauma, fear, and hypervigilance.

# Developmental Stages of Sibling Grief

## Infants and Toddlers

• don't understand death but notice absence and emotional changes

• show distress through behavior changes

## Children (Ages 5–10)

• may think death is reversible

• experience guilt ("Did I cause it?")

• misunderstand medical explanations

## Preteens / Early Adolescents

• understand death but struggle expressing emotions

• may isolate or act out

## Teenagers

• developing independence, so death may derail identity formation

• may turn to friends or avoid grieving at home

• high risk for depression, substance use, or academic decline

## Adults

- may experience the sibling as a part of their identity that is now missing
- often feel responsible for supporting parents
- may feel isolated if their own grief is minimized

## Older Adults

- losing the last sibling can feel like "the end of an era"
- loss of shared childhood memories
- increased awareness of mortality

# Psychological and Emotional Reactions

Sibling grief can be wide-ranging.

## Emotional Reactions

- shock and disbelief
- sadness and longing
- anger at illness, fate, or God
- guilt ("I should have been there")
- jealousy of siblings who remain alive
- numbness or avoidance

## Cognitive Reactions

- intrusive thoughts
- difficulty concentrating
- preoccupation with the circumstances of death
- rumination about the past

## Behavioral Reactions

- withdrawal from family or friends
- aggression or irritability
- risk-taking behaviors
- avoidance of places or memories connected to the sibling

## Physical Reactions

- fatigue
- changes in sleep
- stomachaches or headaches
- weakened immune response

# Complicated Grief in Siblings

Complicated grief, or prolonged grief disorder, occurs when:

- the grief does not ease over time
- functioning becomes impaired
- persistent yearning dominates daily life

Sibling relationships—especially close ones—can heighten the risk.

Signs include:

• intense guilt that doesn't diminish

• avoidance of reminders

• inability to accept the death

• feeling "stuck"

# Family Dynamics After a Sibling Dies

A sibling's death rearranges the family system.

**Impact on Parents**

Parents may withdraw emotionally or be overwhelmed with their own grief.

Siblings may feel:

• ignored

• overshadowed

• pressured to "be good"

### Shifts in Family Roles

Surviving siblings may become:

• the "responsible one"
• the "peacemaker"
• the "silent one"
• the "replacement child"

### Parental Overprotection

Parents may fear losing another child, leading to strict rules, which can frustrate teens or adults.

### The Ghost Sibling

Families may:

• avoid mentioning the deceased
• or talk about them continuously

Either extreme can affect healing.

# Cultural and Spiritual Perspectives

Cultures interpret sibling grief differently.

• African and Caribbean cultures emphasize community mourning
• Native American traditions link siblings spiritually

• Asian cultures often focus on family duty

• Western cultures emphasize personal expression

• religious beliefs (Christianity, Islam, Judaism, etc.) often frame death as transition and may provide comfort

Spiritual views may influence how a sibling understands the loss—whether as punishment, fate, divine will, or a journey.

# Preface

Losing a sibling is a profound and unique form of grief. It is not only the loss of a loved one but the loss of a lifelong companion, a witness to your childhood, and a mirror of your own identity.

This book explores the journey of sibling grief, offering compassionate guidance, emotional insight, and practical strategies for healing.

From the moment everything changes, survivors navigate shock, disbelief, and emotional waves that affect the body, mind, and heart. Sibling grief is often invisible to the outside world, leaving survivors feeling overlooked even as they cope with profound loss. Families are reshaped, roles shift, and unspoken expectations can intensify the emotional burden, but connection and acknowledgment can foster shared healing.

The book addresses the challenges of navigating special dates, milestones, and anniversaries, helping survivors prepare for and honor these moments. It explores the weight of guilt, "what ifs," and the search for meaning, offering strategies to transform regret and questioning into compassion and acceptance.

Rebuilding identity after loss is central to the healing journey. Siblings learn to integrate memories, discover new strengths, and redefine their roles while honoring the legacy of their lost sibling. Healing is nonlinear and ongoing, but over time grief softens, allowing personal growth, resilience, and renewed connection with life.

Ultimately, this book emphasizes that love does not end with death. Through memory, ritual, storytelling, and reflection, survivors can keep their sibling's love alive, creating a lasting legacy that honors both the life lost and the life that continues.

Sibling grief is a journey of enduring love, deep sorrow, and the possibility of growth and hope.

## Overall Themes Across the Book

1. Sibling grief is unique, profound, and often overlooked.

2. Grief affects the body, heart, mind, and family system.

3. Healing is nonlinear, personal, and deeply emotional.

4. Love and memory endure, forming the basis for legacy and meaning-making.

5. Rituals, storytelling, support, and reflection are essential tools for navigating grief.

# Introduction

*Why This Book Exists*

The bond between siblings is like no other. It is a connection built on shared childhoods, family stories, laughter, rivalry, secrets, and unwavering loyalty. Siblings witness each other's growth, joys, and struggles in ways no one else can. Losing a sibling is not just losing a person—it is losing a piece of yourself.

In 2022, I lost my sister, Sandra Faye. Her passing left a hole in my heart that no words could fill. Just as I was beginning to navigate that grief, in 2024, I lost my brother, Jamehl. Losing two siblings within a short span shattered my sense of security, identity, and understanding of the world. I found myself facing grief that was raw, overwhelming, and profoundly isolating.

Through my journey, I realized that the grief of surviving siblings is often overlooked. Society mourns parents and children in the spotlight, but siblings are left carrying a quiet, persistent pain. We are expected to be strong for others, to keep memories alive, to answer questions, and to hold everything together—even when our own hearts feel like they are breaking.

I wrote this book to give voice to that experience. It is a guide, a companion, and a source of comfort for anyone who has lost a brother or sister. Within these pages, you will find personal reflection, practical strategies for coping, insights into the emotional and psychological challenges of sibling loss, and ways to honor the memory of your loved one while continuing to live your own life.

This book is both deeply personal and universally relevant. While it is inspired by my loss of Sandra Faye and Jamehl, it is written for every surviving sibling who has felt the unique pain of losing someone who shaped their life in irreplaceable ways.

My hope is that, through these words, grieving siblings will find understanding, solace, and the courage to navigate their own journeys with compassion and love.

Grief does not have to be carried in silence. Your sibling's memory can live on—not as a weight, but as a guiding presence in your life. This book is here to help you honor that bond, embrace your emotions, and rebuild a life that celebrates both love and resilience.

# Chapter 1:

## *The Moment Everything Changed*

The moment a sibling dies, the world collapses in a way that is difficult to articulate. Life divides itself into two distinct eras: before and after. Even if the loss was expected, even if illness or circumstance prepared the mind, nothing truly prepares the heart.

The moment the news arrives—whether through a phone call, the look on a doctor's face, or the unmistakable silence in the room—everything shifts. Time slows. Reality becomes surreal. The body reacts before the mind can interpret the words. And from that point forward, nothing is ever the same.

Sibling grief begins at the point of impact. It is a shockwave that tears through memory, identity, and the sense of safety that siblings naturally provide. In the early hours and days, grief is not yet shaped; it is raw, disorienting, and overwhelming. Many siblings describe it as an emotional freefall, a loss of gravity, or the feeling of being dropped into an alternate universe where all the rules have changed.

Some people scream. Some collapse. Some go numb. Some detach. But regardless of the immediate reaction, the inner world is shaken beyond recognition.

# The First Wave: Shock and Disbelief

Disbelief is the brain's immediate defense mechanism. Even when the death is confirmed, even when the circumstances are clear, the mind often repeats a silent denial:

*This can't be happening.*
*This isn't real.*
*Not them.*

Shock provides a temporary buffer that allows a grieving sibling to function—calling family members, waiting at the hospital, identifying the body, signing papers, or simply surviving the first 24 hours. Without shock, the emotional weight would be unbearable.

This disbelief is not a sign of weakness; it is a sign of love. Siblings are woven into our everyday existence—our memories, our inside jokes, our shared history. The subconscious simply cannot compute that someone so deeply embedded in the structure of our life is suddenly missing.

Some siblings replay the last moments they saw their brother or sister. Some cling to the final text message. Some replay every detail of the night before, searching for missed signs or clues. Others simply feel trapped in a haze, watching life unfold as if from a distance.

# Frozen Moments That Never Leave

There are certain moments that imprint themselves permanently onto the surviving sibling's memory:

• The sound of the phone ringing

• The crack in a parent's voice

• The sterile hospital room smell

• The stillness of the sibling's hands

• The words the doctor delivered

• The way time seemed to stop, stretch, and collapse all at once

These moments are timeless. They replay months, even years later—not always as pain, but as a reference point. Sibling grief often begins not with the funeral or the weeks after, but with the first moment the heart understood the loss.

---

# When Time Stops and Then Suddenly Accelerates

After the initial shock, many siblings describe a strange contrast: time feels frozen, yet the world around them keeps moving with brutal normalcy.

Cars continue driving. People continue shopping. The sun rises the next day as if nothing happened. Meanwhile, the grieving sibling feels suspended between two realities: the one before the loss and the one they must now navigate without their brother or sister.

Some surviving siblings attempt to power through the early days with mental lists and logistical tasks, trying to provide strength for other family members. Others collapse inward, overwhelmed by the enormity of the void. Both reactions are valid. Both are human responses to trauma.

In this early period, food may have no taste. Sleep becomes fractured. Breathing may feel shallow. Colors seem muted. The world appears dulled, as if seen through fogged glass.

---

## The First Night Without Them

One of the most pivotal emotional experiences is the first night after the loss. The house feels different. The silence is louder.

The absence of footsteps, laughter, or even annoyance becomes deafening. For siblings who shared a home growing up, this night may reopen childhood memories: bunk beds, shared rooms, whispered conversations past bedtime. For siblings who lived separately as adults, the first night might involve sitting alone in the living room staring at nothing, unable to process the fact that their sibling will never walk through the door again.

Sleep offers no real rest. Dreams may be filled with confusion, or the person may wake up repeatedly, forgetting for split seconds and then remembering all over again.

This emotional whiplash is not a flaw—it's a natural part of early grief.

---

# The Search for Meaning in the First Hours

The mind begins to reach for explanation:

Why?
How?
What does this mean for my family?
What does this mean for me?

Human beings are wired to seek patterns, reasons, and order. But death rarely provides them. Sibling loss, in particular, disrupts the perceived map of life. Siblings are supposed to grow old together. They are supposed to be there for milestones, for aging parents, for the next chapter of life.

When that future is abruptly erased, the surviving sibling begins a long internal journey of acceptance and reorientation.

Some siblings turn toward faith. Some turn toward anger. Some turn to silence. Some turn outward, clinging to other loved ones.

All reactions are valid expressions of pain and longing.

---

## Responsibilities That Arrive Before Grief Has Time to Settle

For many siblings, the early hours are filled with responsibilities that must be handled before the emotional processing can begin:

• Contacting family members
• Making funeral plans
• Supporting grieving parents or children
• Securing belongings or personal items
• Answering questions from others
• Managing medical or legal information

These tasks create a strange emotional contradiction—being forced to function while feeling emotionally paralyzed. Some siblings feel guilty for not crying enough. Others feel guilty for crying too much. Some worry they are not being "strong enough," especially if they believe their parents depend on them in this moment. But grief has no correct pace, no correct expression, and no correct order.

---

# Emotional Disorientation

In the first few days, many siblings report:

• Feeling disconnected from their body

• Difficulty focusing or remembering details

• Sudden waves of crying

• Numbness or emotional shutdown

• Sensitivity to loud noises

• A desire to isolate

• A need to talk endlessly about the sibling

• A sense of unreality

This emotional disorientation is not a sign of instability. It is the brain's attempt to protect itself from overload.

---

# When the World Expects You to Be "Okay" Too Soon

One of the earliest challenges of sibling grief is the way the outside world rapidly moves on.

In many cultures, the grief of parents or partners is recognized, but siblings often fall into the background. They may receive fewer calls, fewer check-ins, and fewer outward forms of support.

This creates an emotional divide: the surviving sibling is hurting deeply, but the world may not fully acknowledge the magnitude of the loss.

This lack of acknowledgment does not mean the loss was any less devastating—it simply reflects a societal blind spot that this book will return to throughout.

Sibling grief is profound, and its emotional impact deserves to be honored.

## The Beginning of a Lifelong Journey

The moment everything changed marks not only the beginning of grief but the beginning of transformation.

The surviving sibling will never be the person they were before the loss—but that does not mean they will always be broken.

Healing does not erase the pain; it reshapes it into something survivable, meaningful, and eventually integrated into the story of one's life.

The first chapter of sibling grief is defined by impact, shock, and disorientation. But as the chapters unfold, so does the understanding that grief is not simply about sadness. It is about love. And love does not end with death.

This is where the journey begins—at the moment everything changes.

# Chapter 2:

## *The Bond That Shapes Us*

Siblings are the co-carriers of family history. They are the ones who remember:

- how holidays were celebrated
- what certain relatives were like
- which family stories were exaggerated
- how traditions formed
- what childhood dynamics shaped everyone
- the struggles that outsiders never saw

This shared family legacy creates a sense of grounding. You are not the only one who remembers your grandmother's distinctive laugh, your father's strict rules, or your mother's comforting rituals. Your sibling remembers too. Or remembered.

When a sibling dies, you become the sole witness to pieces of family history that once belonged to two. This can leave a surviving sibling feeling both honored and burdened:

"Now I'm the only one left who remembers."

"Now all those stories live only in me."

"Now I carry the family history alone."

This feeling is emotionally heavy because it shifts the survivor's role from "one of us" to "the last of us" in certain areas of memory. Even if other siblings exist, each relationship is unique—and the memories shared with the lost sibling cannot be duplicated.

## The Emotional Hierarchy of Grief

One of the hardest parts of sibling grief is the emotional hierarchy that society unconsciously builds around loss. When a spouse dies, the community rallies. When a parent dies, everyone understands. But when a sibling dies, the grief is often minimized or dismissed.

People assume:

• parents suffer the most
• spouses suffer profoundly
• children grieve deeply

And they do.

But the sibling's grief is just as real, just as life-altering, and just as enduring. It is simply less acknowledged.

This creates a painful emotional paradox for the surviving sibling. They are grieving deeply, but feel pressured to "stay strong" for others. They may step aside so parents receive the emotional focus. They may feel overshadowed by the grief of a spouse or children. They may feel that expressing their sadness is selfish or inappropriate when others appear to be in more acute pain.

This invisibility intensifies grief. It creates loneliness in a time when connection is most needed. The bond that shaped so much of the survivor's identity becomes a silent loss—one that few understand fully.

## When Siblings Are Best Friends

Some siblings are inseparable. They grow up side by side, sharing every phase of life. They share:

• bedrooms

• schools

• heartbreaks

• secrets

• friends

• dreams

• failures

• spiritual beliefs

• big milestones

They may stay close as adults, talking daily or weekly, checking on one another, helping raise each other's children, going on vacations, celebrating holidays, and offering emotional support.

When this kind of sibling dies, the loss is not only devastating—it is identity-shattering.

The survivor may feel:

• "I lost my best friend."
 • "I lost my other half."
 • "I lost the person who anchored me."
 • "I lost the one who understood me without words."

This depth of grief is immense and deserves full acknowledgment.

# When Siblings Were Not Close — and the Grief Is Still Enormous

Not all sibling relationships are warm or intimate. Some siblings fight constantly. Some grow apart. Some have long periods of estrangement. Some come from chaotic families where survival overshadowed connection. Some simply live different lives.

Yet grief can be just as deep in these cases—sometimes even deeper.

The surviving sibling may experience:

• guilt for the emotional distance
 • regret for opportunities that feel lost forever
 • longing for reconciliation that now cannot happen
 • sorrow for the relationship they wish they had

• confusion about grieving someone with whom the bond was complicated

Grief follows love, but it also follows attachment, history, and identity—even when those connections were painful or imperfect.

## The Bond That Lives in the Body

Modern neuroscience shows that close relationships literally shape the brain. Siblings influence the development of:

• emotional regulation
• communication patterns
• relational instincts
• stress responses
• attachment style

The brain wires itself around the presence of loved ones. It adjusts to their routines, voices, and energy. Over time, the nervous system becomes familiar with their existence.

When a sibling dies, the body reacts as intensely as the mind:

• the nervous system goes into alarm
• sleep cycles change
• appetite fluctuates
• heart rate patterns shift
• cortisol (stress hormone) increases

• safety cues are disrupted

• the body feels disoriented

This physiological impact is part of why sibling grief feels so overwhelming: the body is grieving just as deeply as the mind and heart.

# The Evolution of the Sibling Bond Through Life Stages

Sibling relationships transform through various life phases. Each stage builds unique layers of meaning that deepen grief when a sibling dies.

Early Childhood: Formation
 Siblings are playmates, rivals, companions, and early teachers.

Adolescence: Identity Building
 Siblings either clash or cling, but in both cases they strongly influence self-image.

Young Adulthood: Independence
 Siblings may drift, reconnect, or redefine their relationship.

Adulthood: Partnership
 They may become co-supporters in caring for parents, raising children, building careers, or navigating life challenges.

Later Adulthood: Legacy
 Siblings often reflect together on the past and contemplate the future.

Losing a sibling at any stage disrupts the emotional timeline—but losing them in adulthood or later life has profound symbolic meaning. It erases part of a shared future.

## The Sibling as a Lifelong Witness

One of the most sacred roles a sibling plays is that of witness. They see each other evolve from childhood innocence to adult complexity. They know:

• who you were before heartbreak

• who you were before responsibilities

• who you were before trauma

• who you became afterward

A sibling has memory fragments that include you. They hold pieces of your life that no one else does. When they die, the remaining sibling may feel as though a part of their life story vanished.

Many people describe this as:

"No one else remembers me the way they did."

"I lost the person who knew my whole life."

"It feels like part of my story died with them."

This is not merely emotional; it is existential. Losing a sibling disrupts the sense of being known.

# A Bond That Death Cannot Take

Despite grief, separation, or physical death, the sibling bond does not end. It evolves.

Many survivors report:

• dreaming of their sibling

• sensing their presence

• feeling guided or protected

• maintaining rituals or traditions

• talking to them internally

• carrying their traits or values forward

• seeing them reflected in their children

• feeling their influence in daily choices

Love does not leave. Connection does not disappear. The bond remains—transformed, quieter, but enduring.

This continued bond becomes one of the most important healing forces for surviving siblings. It creates meaning, comfort, and a sense of ongoing relationship that helps the heart integrate the loss into a new narrative.

# Conclusion of Chapter 2

The sibling bond—whether warm, distant, complicated, or inseparable—shapes identity, memory, and emotional development in profound ways. This is why sibling grief is so deep, so layered, and so often misunderstood. The bond is unique. The love is unique. And therefore, the grief is unique.

Sibling loss is not simply the loss of a person. It is the loss of a witness, a companion, a mirror, and a piece of the self. Understanding this bond is essential to understanding the journey that follows.

Sibling relationships are unique and lifelong. They shape personality, identity, and emotional growth. This bond is often the first peer-like relationship a child experiences, filled with shared experiences, competition, support, and love.

Loss of a sibling disrupts this lifelong connection, affecting how survivors view themselves and the world. Even distant or complicated relationships leave a deep emotional imprint, making grief multifaceted and complex.

The bond between siblings is unlike any other relationship. It is often the longest relationship of a person's life—beginning in childhood, lasting through adolescence, adulthood, and sometimes old age. Even when a sibling relationship is complicated, distant, or strained, it shapes who we become in ways we don't always realize until the bond is broken.

Siblings are the people who witness our entire story. They know the version of us that existed long before the world had expectations. They know the secrets of our family, the rhythms of our childhood home, the unspoken rules, the inside jokes, the scars and the victories. They know the way our mother sighed when she was tired, or how our father drove too fast, or how holidays felt in the house we grew up in. They knew our laugh before it changed with age. They knew our face before grief touched it.

This shared history is why sibling grief cuts so deeply—because it is not just the loss of a person, but the loss of a mirror, a witness, a keeper of memory.

Some siblings were inseparable—sharing rooms, toys, dreams, and secrets. They fought and made up, broke things and blamed each other, helped each other through heartbreak, encouraged each other through milestones, and dreamed together about the future. For these siblings, the loss feels like losing a best friend, a lifelong companion, a part of the soul that doesn't regenerate.

Other siblings were bonded through protection—one more nurturing, one more rebellious, one older and guiding, one younger and looking up with admiration. Even if life separated them later on, that early imprint remains. When a protective sibling dies, the surviving one may feel unanchored, as though the person who steadied them is suddenly gone.

Some siblings had complicated relationships—arguments, distance, or tension that never fully healed. When such a sibling dies, the grief can feel tangled: mourning what was, what wasn't, and what could have been. Regret, confusion, guilt, sadness, anger, and longing can weave together in a way that is especially painful. This too is love—love that didn't have space or time to express itself fully.

There are also siblings who drifted apart unintentionally. Life moved quickly. Careers, children, relationships, and responsibilities piled up. Texts became less frequent. Visits became harder to arrange. When the loss happens, the surviving sibling may ache for the time they didn't make, or the conversations they thought they'd have someday. The grief becomes a collision between love and lost time.

Yet no matter the type of relationship, the bond is profound. Whether tender or complicated, it shapes identity. Sibling dynamics influence confidence, fears, communication patterns, and the way we approach the world. Losing that presence feels like losing a part of the foundation beneath our feet.

Many people say, "I didn't realize how much my sibling meant to me until they were gone." This is not a failure—it is the nature of lifelong relationships. We grow accustomed to certain people being part of the backdrop of our world. We assume they will always be there, even when life keeps us busy. Their presence feels like a constant, woven into everyday existence.

When that constant disappears, the silence is loud. The world suddenly feels different—less familiar, less safe, less shared. Surviving siblings often feel a shift inside themselves, as if a thread that held together their understanding of who they are has been quietly pulled loose.

But even in grief, the bond does not vanish. It transforms. Love becomes memory. Connection becomes grief. Presence becomes legacy.

And little by little, the surviving sibling learns how to carry both the love and the loss together.

The chapters ahead will explore this transformation—how grief shows up in the body and mind, how family systems shift after a loss, how guilt and "what ifs" settle into the heart, and how healing begins even when it feels impossible.

But it all begins with this truth:

Sibling bonds shape us—and losing a sibling reshapes us forever.

# Chapter 3:

*When the World Doesn't Understand*

WHEN THE CALL COMES: THE MOMENT EVERYTHING CHANGES

There are moments in life that divide time into two parts: before and after. The birth of a child, the signing of a marriage certificate, a spiritual awakening, a sudden illness, a profound success. But nothing redraws the landscape of a person's soul quite like the moment they learn that a sibling has died.

This moment—the call, the knock on the door, the message, the trembling voice on the other end—is often described as surreal, disorienting, and permanently life-altering. It is the kind of moment that freezes itself in memory, replaying for years, sometimes decades.

This chapter explores the emotional shock, the physical impact, and the psychological rupture that occurs when the news first reaches the surviving sibling.

# The World Tilts: First Awareness of Loss

Grief often begins with confusion rather than clarity. The first words a person hears after a sibling's death rarely make full sense. They come through muffled, distorted, as if entering through water.

People often say:

- "It felt like everything around me stopped."
- "I heard the words, but my mind rejected them."
- "I kept saying, 'No, that's not right.'"
- "I thought it was a mistake."

Denial is not a failure to accept reality. It is the body's instinctive attempt to protect the mind from overwhelming shock. It gives you time to breathe before the truth fully lands.

# The Body Reacts Before the Mind Understands

Long before the mind processes what has happened, the body reacts.

Survivors often report:

- sudden weakness in the knees
- shaking hands
- chest pressure or rapid heartbeats
- numbness or tingling
- nausea or vomiting

- fainting or feeling lightheaded

- immediate tears or complete emotional numbness

- a feeling of "dropping" or sinking internally

This is because the nervous system goes into acute shock. Adrenaline surges. The body tries to brace itself against emotional collapse.

This reaction is not dramatic or unusual; it is human physiology responding to devastating news.

## The Moment of Disbelief

Whether the relationship was close, complicated, distant, or still developing, the disbelief is almost universal.

Siblings often think:

- "I just talked to them."
- "There's no way this is real."
- "Someone must be mistaken."
- "This can't be happening to us."

Disbelief is not denial—it is a natural attempt to reconcile the brain's expectations with sudden reality. Your mind knew your sibling as alive. It had no time to adjust. The news creates a violent contradiction inside the psyche.

# The Overwhelming Rush of Memory

Almost instantly, memories begin surfacing—some clear, some fragmented. Childhood images, moments of laughter, arguments, holidays, secrets, old fights, old forgiveness. The mind frantically searches for something—connection, meaning, last conversations.

Some describe it as:

• a mental slideshow
• a rush of moments both big and small
• flashes of early childhood
• the last thing the sibling said
• regrets that suddenly feel enormous
• precious memories that return with unexpected force

In this moment, time becomes fluid. The past feels closer than the present.

# The Sibling Role Breaks Open

When the news arrives, the surviving sibling's role shifts instantly—even if they are not ready.

They may now become:

• the one who breaks the news to others
• the emotional anchor for grieving parents
• the communicator for extended family

- the organizer of immediate logistics

- the supporter of the sibling's children or partner

- the person everyone looks to for information

This can create immense internal conflict.

On the outside, they must function. On the inside, they are breaking.

Many siblings describe it as: "I went into autopilot." "My body did things while my heart was somewhere else." "I was comforting everyone while I felt like screaming."

## The Emotional Reactions That Follow

Shortly after the news hits, emotional shock often fragments into waves—sharp, unpredictable, and difficult to control.

1.  Numbness

    A sense of emotional emptiness, as if the world has gone quiet.

2.  Panic

    Fear of the unknown—what happened, what comes next, what life will look like.

3.  Desperation

    Wishing desperately for it to be reversible, praying for a miracle.

4.  Guilt

Immediate regrets surface:

- "I should have called more."
- "I should have visited."
- "Our last conversation wasn't perfect."

Guilt is common, and it does not mean the relationship was flawed. It means the love was real.

5.  Anger

At the situation, the world, the unfairness, or even at the sibling for leaving.

6.  Disorientation

Time feels strange. Hours pass without awareness.

7.  Protectiveness

Many siblings instantly worry about their parents, children, or the deceased sibling's partner.

These reactions are normal. They are the psyche's attempt to understand a devastating blow.

# The Practical Demands Clash With Emotional Reality

There is a painful irony in the hours after losing a sibling: the world expects decisions at the exact moment when the grief is strongest.

Survivors may have to:

- call family members
- speak with doctors
- make or assist with funeral decisions
- check on children or spouses
- gather personal items
- handle paperwork

These tasks clash violently with emotional reality.

A person may be thinking: "I don't even believe this is real—how am I making decisions?"

Yet somehow, the tasks get done. And this creates a strange guilt later, because the mind thinks it should have collapsed, but instead it functioned.

You did not fail your sibling by being functional. You were surviving something unimaginable.

# The First Night: The Longest Hours

The first night after the news is often described as impossible, painfully quiet, filled with disbelief, sleepless, overwhelming, and full of questions with no answers.

Many siblings report:

- staring into space
- replaying the news repeatedly
- pacing or restless movement
- tears that come in waves
- sudden jolts of panic
- moments of remembering and forgetting
- feeling the bed is physically too big
- sensing the sibling's absence like a heavy weight

This night becomes etched into memory, forming the emotional imprint of the loss.

# When the Relationship Was Complicated

If the sibling relationship had distance, disagreements, unresolved conflict, or emotional complexity, the news hits with an extra layer of pain.

Survivors may feel:

• guilt

• relief (followed by guilt for feeling relief)

• sadness for what could have been

• longing for reconciliation

• confusion

• shame for not being closer

• anger at the circumstances

But complicated love is still love. Complicated relationships still produce deep grief. There is no "right" type of sibling relationship required for heartbreak.

## The Moment You Realize Nothing Will Ever Be the Same

At some point—hours, days, or weeks later—the truth settles deeper. It is no longer just information. It becomes reality.

This realization often comes with:

• a wave of grief that feels like it breaks the body

• a moment of collapsing emotionally

• a deeper level of acceptance that feels unbearable

• a sense of life being permanently altered

It's the moment you think: "This is real. My sibling is truly gone."

And with that realization comes the beginning of the long, complex process of coping, healing, remembering, and rebuilding.

# Conclusion of Chapter 3

The moment the news arrives is a psychological earthquake. It splits the world into a before and after. It shakes one's identity, body, memory, and reality. It marks the beginning of a journey no one is prepared to walk.

Sibling loss is not just the death of a family member. It is the collapse of a shared history, a shift in identity, and the birth of a grief that touches every part of life.

And yet, even in this moment of devastating shock, the seeds of healing, connection, and transformation quietly begin to form.

Sibling grief is often invisible. Society tends to focus on parental or spousal grief, leaving surviving siblings feeling overlooked. Friends, coworkers, and even family members may minimize the loss.

Survivors need acknowledgment of their grief to validate their experience. Hidden grief can exacerbate loneliness and emotional isolation, emphasizing the importance of support, communication, and understanding.

One of the most painful parts of losing a sibling is discovering how invisible the grief can feel. The world has rituals and language for losing a parent, a child, or a spouse. But sibling grief often receives far less recognition, even though the loss can be just as devastating, just as life-altering.

Many siblings describe feeling overlooked in the earliest days after the death. Friends ask how the parents are holding up. Extended family members gather around the spouse or children of the one who passed. Community members send meals, cards, and support—but often direct it toward the "primary mourners."

The sibling stands somewhere in the middle, fully shattered but expected to be strong. Expected to help. Expected to hold the rest of the family together.

People don't always realize that siblings are grieving too—deeply, fiercely, quietly.

This invisibility can make the loss feel even heavier. It creates an ache that comes from mourning alone in a room full of people who are also grieving. Even when others mean well, their focus may unintentionally shift away from the sibling, leaving them feeling forgotten in their own grief story.

In many families, siblings take on roles immediately after the loss—caring for parents, making arrangements, contacting relatives, cleaning out belongings, or helping with younger family members. While they move through these tasks, their own heartbreak gets pushed inward.

Later, long after the funeral is over and people stop checking in, the grief rises again, often intensified by the sense that no one ever fully saw their pain.

This kind of "hidden grief" can show up in surprising ways:

- Feeling guilty for wanting support
- Believing they have no right to be devastated
- Feeling unrecognized or "less important"
- Anger that their relationship is minimized
- Confusion about where they fit in the family now
- Withdrawing emotionally because no one understands

But sibling grief is real. And it deserves space.

Siblings often carry the unique burden of shared history—they are the people who remember your earliest stories, your childhood home, your growing pains, your family's secrets, your jokes, your scars, your triumphs. Losing the person who walked through those memories with you is not small. It is not secondary. It is not less significant.

Siblings also carry the future-oriented grief—the lost time they thought they would have together. The future children their sibling won't meet. The birthdays, holidays, graduations, and milestones that will feel different forever. The person they imagined growing old with, reminiscing with, laughing about the past with—gone.

But because society often lacks rituals for siblings, their grief becomes quieter. They may feel pressure to "stay strong," to avoid upsetting others, or to keep the family moving forward.

This quietness can turn grief into loneliness, even in a house full of people.

Many siblings say things like: "I didn't feel like I was allowed to grieve." "Everyone kept checking on my parents, but no one checked on me." "I felt guilty for crying when I knew my mom was hurting more." "I became the strong one, but inside I was falling apart."

This chapter exists to make one truth clear:

Sibling grief is profound, valid, and deserving of care.

Your relationship with your sibling was real—whether it was easy or complicated, close or distant, lifelong or evolving. Your love had a shape. Your connection had a story. Your grief is part of that story, and it matters.

In the chapters ahead, we will explore not only the emotions of loss but also the ways grief affects the body, the mind, and the spirit. We will talk about the family shifts that follow the death of a sibling—the changes in roles, communication, closeness, and conflict. And we will look at the healing journey that unfolds slowly, quietly, and beautifully over time.

But before all of that, you deserve this acknowledgment:

You are grieving.

Your grief is real.

Your grief is worthy of recognition.

# Chapter 4:

*Grief in the Body, Heart, and Mind*

THE COMPLEX LANDSCAPE OF SIBLING GRIEF

Sibling grief is deep, layered, and often misunderstood. It is one of the most complex forms of bereavement because siblings occupy emotional territory that no one else in life touches. They are our first peers, our co-authors of childhood, our rivals, protectors, confidants, and mirrors. They shape who we are long before the world has a voice in the matter.

When a sibling dies, the grief reverberates through identity, memory, family systems, and the self in ways most people never anticipate. This chapter examines those complexities—emotional, psychological, relational, and developmental—so that readers can better understand what they are experiencing or supporting in others.

## Why Sibling Grief Is Deeply Unique

Sibling grief differs from the death of a parent, a child, or a partner. It occupies a category of its own because:

1. Siblings Share the Longest Relationships of Our Lives
    Most siblings are present from early childhood and remain

throughout decades of major milestones. This continuity builds powerful bonds that are difficult to articulate.

2. They Are Witnesses to Our Life Story

    Siblings often know:

• where we came from

• how we grew up

• what shaped us

• the secrets we hold

• the hardships our family faced

No one else shares the full backdrop of our formative years.

3. Sibling Loss Alters Identity

    Losing a sibling is more than losing a relationship—it is losing a piece of yourself, of who you have always been. The internal question becomes: "Who am I now without them?"

4. The Loss Is Often Minimized by Society

    Friends, coworkers, or extended family may unintentionally diminish the grief by focusing primarily on parents or spouses. This can leave the surviving sibling feeling invisible.

# The Emotional Complexity of Sibling Grief

Sibling grief is rarely one-dimensional. It contains a spectrum of emotions that can coexist, contradict, and overlap.

1.  Deep Love and Deep Pain

    Even in conflicted sibling relationships, love runs deep. So does the pain of losing someone who shaped your entire life story.

2.  Regret and Unfinished Business

    Siblings often feel:

• guilt over past arguments

• regret about distance

• concern over things left unsaid

• shame about unresolved tension

Even close relationships carry moments that feel heavy after death.

3.  Loneliness That Is Hard to Explain

    Sibling grief creates a distinct loneliness. It's:

• the loss of someone who shared your childhood bed

• the silence of no longer having someone who "gets" your upbringing

• the absence of a familiar voice you expected to hear forever

It is loneliness rooted in memory and identity.

4.  Relief Mixed With Guilt (In Certain Situations)
    If a sibling suffered from addiction, illness, or conflict, the
    surviving sibling may feel a strange mixture of sadness and relief.
    This is a normal grief reaction, not a disrespect to the sibling's
    memory.

5.  Anger at the Unfairness of It All
    The anger may be directed at:

• the circumstances

• God

• fate

• medical professionals

• the sibling (for leaving)

• themselves

Anger is not a sign of weakness or immaturity—it is a valid stage of grief.

# The Developmental Layers of Sibling Loss

Sibling grief manifests differently depending on:

- the sibling's age
- the survivor's age
- the stage of life
- the emotional closeness
- the family structure

## Losing a Sibling in Childhood

The surviving child may experience:

- confusion
- fear of losing other family members
- sudden maturity
- guilt for surviving
- anxiety
- changes in behavior or performance

Children often grieve in waves, revisiting the loss as they grow older and understand death differently.

## Losing a Sibling in Young Adulthood

This stage of life is already filled with transitions. Losing a sibling can lead to:

- disrupted dreams
- fear of the future

- identity instability
- feeling robbed of adult friendship with the sibling

It can intensify feelings of isolation among peers.

## Losing a Sibling in Midlife

This often brings:

- grief mixed with responsibility
- pressure to support aging parents
- a reminder of mortality
- shifts in family roles
- deep reflection on life choices

The sibling becomes a link between generational identity and present responsibilities.

## Losing a Sibling in Older Age

For older adults, sibling loss can trigger:

- fear of being the "last one left"
- reflection on childhood memories
- existential questions
- grief intertwined with nostalgia
- the collapse of shared history

Siblings at this stage are often the only remaining witnesses to earlier decades.

# How Sibling Relationships Shape Grief

Because no two sibling relationships are identical, grief can take many forms.

## 1. The Protective Older Sibling

The surviving older sibling may feel:

- guilt for not preventing the death
- responsibility to care for parents
- the collapse of their "protector" identity

They may feel emotionally torn between their own grief and their duty to others.

## 2. The Younger Sibling

Younger siblings often experience:

- loss of guidance
- feeling unanchored
- fear
- the collapse of a figure they idealized
- sudden emotional maturity

They may grieve not only the sibling's death but the future guidance they will never receive.

## 3. The "Twin Energy" Dynamic

Even for non-twins, some siblings share deep synchrony. The loss feels like:

- losing a piece of one's self
- losing a mirror
- losing a life partner of sorts
- losing the person who "just knew"

The grief is profound and often misunderstood by others.

## 4. The Sibling Who Was Also a Best Friend

This grief is multi-layered:

- losing a confidant
- losing companionship
- losing emotional safety
- losing part of daily life

The survivor may struggle deeply with loneliness.

## 5. The Estranged or Distant Sibling

This grief carries:

- guilt

- regret

- confusion

- longing

- unresolved pain

It does not mean the grief is lesser. In fact, unresolved relationships often create more complex grief.

# The Family System After a Sibling's Death

Sibling loss is not an isolated experience. It disrupts the entire family system.

## Parents May Become Emotionally Unavailable

Parents in deep grief may unintentionally neglect the surviving children. This can create feelings of invisibility.

## Family Roles Shift

The surviving sibling may suddenly become:

- the emotional support

- the peacemaker

- the communicator

- the representative at events

- the "strong one"

These roles can be overwhelming.

**Birth Order Gets Redefined**

If the oldest dies, the middle becomes the oldest. If the youngest dies, the middle becomes the youngest. These shifts affect identity and responsibility.

**Family Gatherings Change**

Holidays, birthdays, reunions, and traditions will never feel the same. There is always a missing chair, a missing laugh, a missing presence.

# Isolation: The Invisible Burden of Sibling Grief

One of the greatest challenges is the feeling of being unseen.

People may unintentionally say:

• "Your parents must be devastated."
• "How is their spouse doing?"
• "At least you still have your own life."

Rarely does someone say: "How are you doing with losing your sibling?"

This societal minimization can lead to:

• emotional isolation
• internalized pain

- suppressed grief

- resentment

- feeling "unentitled" to grieve

Sibling grief deserves recognition and support. It is real. It is deep. It is life-changing.

## The Myth That Siblings Should "Be Strong"

Surviving siblings often feel pressure to carry the emotional load:

- supporting parents
- helping with arrangements
- comforting nieces and nephews
- explaining the loss to others

This pressure can push their own grief into the background.

Being strong does not mean being untouched. Strength can coexist with heartbreak, tears, and vulnerability.

## The Identity Crisis That Follows Loss

Sibling loss destabilizes identity because siblings shape:

- how we see ourselves
- where we fit in the family
- our memories
- our personality
- our sense of continuity

When they are gone, the internal question becomes: "Who was I with them?" "Who am I now without them?"

Identity reconstruction becomes part of the healing journey.

# Conclusion of Chapter 4

Sibling grief is complex because the relationship itself is complex—rich with history, conflict, love, rivalry, companionship, and identity. It is grief that touches every part of a person's life and reshapes the internal world permanently.

Understanding this complexity is essential. Not to make grief easier—because it can never be simplified—but to make it less lonely.

Grief affects the body, mind, and heart simultaneously. Physical symptoms may include fatigue, chest tightness, headaches, and sleep disturbances. Emotionally, grief brings sadness, anger, longing, and confusion. Mentally, survivors may experience fog, intrusive thoughts, and difficulty concentrating.

Understanding grief as a whole-body experience helps siblings navigate these reactions with patience, self-compassion, and awareness.

Grief is not just an emotion—it is a physical, mental, and spiritual event that moves through the entire body. Losing a sibling can create sensations and reactions that feel confusing, overwhelming, or even frightening, especially when they appear without warning.

Many people believe grief is only about sadness. But sibling grief is far more complex. It is exhaustion, confusion, longing, anger, fog, fear, numbness, aching, and love all woven together. It is a whole-body experience.

The body remembers what the heart can't explain. The body reacts to grief before the mind has even processed what happened. Some siblings describe feeling shaky, lightheaded, or unable to breathe when they first hear the news. Others feel heavy, as if gravity suddenly doubled.

In the days and weeks that follow, physical symptoms often appear:

- tightness in the chest
- loss of appetite or overeating
- headaches
- stomach pain
- difficulty sleeping or sleeping too much
- feeling weak or drained

- a sense of pressure or heaviness in the body
- sudden bursts of adrenaline or panic

These reactions are the body's survival system responding to emotional trauma. The loss of a sibling is not only heartbreaking—it is destabilizing. It shakes the nervous system because it touches something primal: family, identity, memory, and safety.

The heart holds the longing. Emotional grief is not linear. It rises, falls, circles, pauses, and returns when you least expect it. One moment you may feel steady, and the next you may be hit with a wave so strong it takes your breath away.

Sibling grief often carries layers that other losses do not: a longing for shared history, a longing for future moments, and a longing for their presence. The heart aches for the person who grew beside you—the one who knew your childhood without you having to explain it.

Sometimes the heartbreak shows up as sadness, and other times as irritability, restlessness, emotional numbness, weeping without knowing why, feeling lost or unanchored, or sudden bursts of anger or frustration. These reactions are normal. They are part of the heart's attempt to adjust to a world that feels wrong without your sibling in it.

# Chapter 5:

*The Family That Remains*

When a sibling dies, the loss does not affect only one person. It reshapes the entire family system. Each family member grieves differently, and those differences can create confusion, distance, or unexpected closeness. The death of a sibling changes how people relate to one another, how responsibilities are shared, and how the family sees itself moving forward.

Families are living systems. Every member plays a role, and when one person disappears, the balance shifts. Surviving siblings often feel this shift immediately. The family they knew—the emotional rhythm, the interactions, the sense of completeness—has changed forever.

## Grief Looks Different for Everyone

One of the first challenges surviving siblings notice is that grief rarely looks the same for two people. Even individuals who loved the same person deeply may express their grief in completely different ways.

Some family members cry openly. Others become quiet and withdrawn. Some want to talk about the person who died constantly, while others avoid the topic because it hurts too much. Some find comfort in memories and storytelling, while others focus on practical tasks to keep moving forward.

These differences can create misunderstanding. A sibling may think, "Why aren't they talking about them?" or "Why do they seem okay?" But grief is deeply personal. It is shaped by personality, life experiences, coping styles, and the nature of the relationship with the person who died.

Recognizing these differences can help prevent resentment or misinterpretation within the family.

## The Grief of Parents

For many surviving siblings, one of the most painful parts of the loss is witnessing their parents' grief. Parents often experience a level of devastation that is difficult to watch. The death of a child can shatter a parent's sense of identity, purpose, and protection.

Surviving siblings may feel a deep urge to protect their parents from additional pain. They may try to hide their own grief in order to appear strong. They may become caretakers, emotional supporters, or problem-solvers within the family.

While this instinct comes from love, it can also place an enormous burden on the surviving sibling. Carrying both personal grief and the desire to protect others can become emotionally exhausting.

It is important to remember that siblings are grieving too. Their pain deserves space and recognition, even while the family navigates the parents' heartbreak.

## When Parents Become Emotionally Distant

In some families, parents become emotionally distant after the loss of a child. Their grief may be so overwhelming that they withdraw from conversations, routines, or emotional connection.

Surviving siblings may interpret this distance in painful ways. They may feel forgotten, unimportant, or invisible. They may wonder if their parents are so consumed by the loss that they cannot see the child who is still here.

Often, this distance is not intentional. It is a sign of deep grief and emotional exhaustion. Parents who have lost a child may struggle to find the energy or clarity needed to engage with the world the way they once did.

Understanding this can help siblings avoid internalizing the distance as rejection, though the emotional impact may still be difficult.

## Shifts in Family Roles

The death of a sibling often causes immediate shifts in family roles. Responsibilities that once belonged to one person may suddenly fall to someone else.

A sibling who once felt carefree may now feel responsible for supporting parents or maintaining family stability. A quieter sibling may find themselves speaking up more often. A younger sibling may feel pressure to grow up quickly.

Some siblings describe feeling as though they must now "fill the space" left behind. They may try to take on characteristics of the sibling who died or feel pressure to succeed in ways that honor the family's expectations.

These shifts can create internal conflict. The surviving sibling may feel torn between their authentic self and the role they believe the family now needs them to play.

## The Pressure to Be the Strong One

In many families, surviving siblings become the "strong one." They handle logistics, communicate with relatives, comfort grieving family members, and keep daily life moving forward.

While strength can be admirable, it can also become isolating. The sibling who appears strong may not receive the same level of emotional support as others. People may assume they are coping well simply because they are functioning.

Inside, however, that sibling may feel overwhelmed, exhausted, or unseen.

Strength should never require someone to hide their pain. Even the most resilient individuals need space to grieve, cry, and be supported.

# Changes in Sibling Relationships

If multiple siblings remain, their relationships may change in unexpected ways after the loss.

Some siblings grow closer. Shared grief can deepen bonds, creating a sense of unity and mutual understanding.

Other siblings may drift apart. Differences in grieving styles, communication patterns, or emotional needs can create tension.

Neither outcome is unusual. Families adjust to loss in complex ways, and sibling relationships may evolve over time as each person processes the grief differently.

Maintaining open communication can help siblings support one another, even when their experiences of grief are not identical.

# The Silence That Sometimes Follows

After the funeral and the initial wave of support passes, families often return to everyday life. Work resumes. School continues. Responsibilities return.

Yet something fundamental has changed.

Sometimes families stop talking about the sibling who died because the pain feels too intense. The name is mentioned less frequently. Memories are shared less often.

For surviving siblings, this silence can feel painful. They may worry that speaking about the sibling will upset others. They may feel that their memories are being quietly set aside.

Remembering a sibling should not be seen as reopening a wound. For many people, sharing stories and memories becomes an important part of healing.

## The Empty Chair

Family gatherings often make the absence most visible. Holidays, birthdays, graduations, and anniversaries highlight the space where someone once sat.

Surviving siblings may notice the empty chair at the table, the missing laugh during conversations, or the absence of familiar traditions.

These moments can trigger waves of grief even years after the loss. They serve as reminders that the family structure has changed.

At the same time, families sometimes create new traditions to honor the sibling's memory. Lighting a candle, sharing stories, or acknowledging their presence during special occasions can help keep the connection alive.

# Navigating Family Expectations

Families sometimes develop unspoken expectations after a loss. A sibling may feel pressure to live in a way that honors the person who died. They may feel expected to succeed, to stay close to home, or to fulfill responsibilities once shared by the sibling.

These expectations may come from love and grief rather than direct demands. Still, they can create emotional pressure.

It is important for surviving siblings to remember that honoring a loved one does not require losing themselves. Each person must continue living their own life while carrying the memory of the sibling forward.

# Finding New Balance

Over time, families gradually adjust to the new reality created by loss. This does not mean the grief disappears. Rather, the family begins to find a different rhythm.

Conversations slowly return. Shared experiences rebuild connection. New memories form alongside the old ones.

The sibling who died remains part of the family story, even though their physical presence is gone.

Families learn to carry both grief and love at the same time.

# Conclusion of Chapter 5

The death of a sibling reshapes the family that remains. Relationships shift, roles evolve, and emotional dynamics change. Surviving siblings often find themselves navigating their own grief while also responding to the needs of parents, relatives, and other family members.

Understanding these shifts can help reduce confusion and isolation. It reminds surviving siblings that the changes they experience are part of the natural process of adjusting to profound loss.

Although the family will never be the same, it can still find ways to heal, support one another, and keep the memory of the sibling alive within its shared story.

# Chapter 6:

*Navigating Special Dates and Difficult Days*

WHEN THE WORLD EXPECTS YOU TO BE STRONG

In the wake of a sibling's death, there is a powerful—and often unfair—expectation placed on the surviving sibling: to be strong. To hold the family together. To handle the details. To ease the burden for everyone else. To push aside personal grief and rise to the moment.

The world may not say these words aloud, but the message is implied in the way people respond. Siblings often find themselves praised for composure they never intended to display, for strength they never chose, and for resilience that costs them deeply.

This chapter explores the external pressures and internal conflicts created by these expectations and how they shape the experience of sibling grief.

## The Unspoken Assignment: "Be the Strong One"

When death enters a family, everyone is thrown into emotional chaos. Parents may collapse under the weight of losing a child. Spouses may break down in shock. Children may have no understanding of what has happened.

In this emotional vacuum, the surviving sibling often becomes the default leader of the grieving process.

This role is not assigned verbally.

It emerges silently.

You may notice:

• people look to you to make decisions
• you're the one answering calls and messages
• family asks you what "should" happen next
• relatives say you're "handling everything so well"
• you're told, "Your parents need you right now"
• no one asks if you need support

This silent expectation can be overwhelming, especially when you are barely holding yourself together.

## Why Siblings Are Expected to Be Strong

There are several reasons society leans on siblings in this way:

1. To Protect Grieving Parents

People instinctively believe that parents suffer the deepest grief. This may be true emotionally, but it does not reduce the sibling's pain. Still, siblings often hide their grief to "spare" their parents.

2.  Because Siblings Often Understand the Family Structure

Siblings know how the family operates, who communicates with whom, and what needs to be done. This familiarity leads others to rely on them heavily.

3.  Because People Underestimate Sibling Bonds

Many assume sibling relationships are less emotionally significant than parent–child or spouse relationships. This misconception leads to unrealistic expectations of resilience.

4.  Because Siblings Often Internalize Responsibility

Growing up, siblings protect, cover for, defend, or rescue each other. That instinct can carry into adulthood—creating a sense of responsibility even after death.

5.  Cultural or Familial Roles

In many families, the oldest sibling or the most emotionally stable sibling naturally becomes the one others depend on.

Regardless of the reason, the expectation creates pressure that shapes the entire grieving experience.

# The Mask of Composure

Siblings often feel compelled to hold themselves together in front of others. They become:

- the organizer
- the communicator
- the planner
- the listener
- the mediator
- the emotional anchor

This leads to the creation of a "mask"—a composed exterior that hides a storm underneath.

# The Mask Provides Protection—but at a Cost

The mask of strength:

- protects parents
- stabilizes a chaotic situation

* reassures extended family

* helps manage logistics

But it also:

* suppresses emotions

* delays personal grief

* causes emotional exhaustion

* creates resentment

* increases isolation

* leads to breakdowns when alone

The mask may keep others calm, but internally the sibling is drowning.

## The Conflict Between Duty and Pain

Surviving siblings often experience a painful internal conflict: the duty to be strong versus the need to grieve.

Examples include:

* comforting a crying parent while wanting to collapse inside
* helping plan a funeral while feeling unable to think clearly
* sitting beside a grieving spouse while feeling equally lost
* supporting nieces or nephews while longing for support themselves

This conflict forces siblings to divide themselves emotionally:

* one part functioning
* one part grieving
* one part soothing others

This division is draining and unsustainable, yet many siblings have no choice in the moment.

# The Emotional Labor Hidden Behind Strength

"Strength" in grief is not just a posture—it is labor. Emotional labor.

Siblings quietly handle tasks that others overlook.

## 1. Answering painful questions repeatedly

People ask:

"What happened?"
"How are your parents?"
"Are you holding up?"

These questions reopen wounds each time.

## 2. Protecting family members from additional pain

Siblings filter information, soften bad news, and hide upsetting details.

## 3. Mediating family conflicts

Tension often rises under grief. Siblings smooth over disagreements about:

- funeral decisions
- estate matters
- personal belongings
- memories or interpretations of events
- who "should" be involved

## 4. Maintaining normalcy

Siblings try to keep routines, especially when children are involved.

## 5. Carrying everyone else's emotions

They often absorb the tears, fears, and anger of others.

This emotional weight compounds the personal grief they are already experiencing.

# Chapter 7:

*The Weight of "What If" and "Why"*

After the shock of losing a sibling begins to settle, many survivors enter a painful mental landscape filled with questions. These questions often circle endlessly through the mind, searching for explanations that may never fully exist.

Why did this happen?
Could something have been different?
Did I miss a sign?
Could I have stopped it?

These questions form the heavy burden of "what if" and "why." They are a natural response to loss, yet they can trap grieving siblings in cycles of guilt, regret, and relentless mental replay.

This chapter explores the emotional and psychological impact of these questions and how survivors can gradually move from self-blame toward compassion and acceptance.

# The Mind's Search for Meaning

Human beings are wired to search for cause and effect. When something devastating happens, the mind instinctively tries to understand why.

In everyday life, this ability helps people solve problems and avoid danger. But in grief, this same instinct can become painful and exhausting.

Sibling loss often creates questions that have no clear answers. The mind struggles with the lack of control, and so it begins to reconstruct the past—examining conversations, decisions, and moments that now feel significant.

Surviving siblings may replay events repeatedly:

- the last phone call
- the last visit
- the last argument
- the last text message
- the last time they saw their sibling alive

Each memory becomes a potential turning point in the mind's attempt to change the outcome.

# The Loop of "What If"

"What if" questions are one of the most common experiences in sibling grief.

People often think:

What if I had called sooner?

What if I had visited more often?

What if I had said something different?

What if I had noticed something was wrong?

These questions are not truly about facts. They are expressions of love and longing. The mind imagines alternate timelines where the sibling is still alive.

But the reality is that grief cannot be solved through logic. The past cannot be rewritten, no matter how many times the mind replays it.

## Guilt and Responsibility

Many siblings carry a sense of responsibility after a loss, even when they had no control over what happened.

This guilt can appear in many forms:

• guilt for surviving
• guilt for not preventing the death
• guilt for arguments or distance in the past
• guilt for moments of relief if the sibling suffered from illness or addiction
• guilt for moving forward with life

These feelings are common in grief, yet they can become overwhelming if left unexamined.

It is important to understand that guilt often arises because the relationship mattered deeply. The mind wants to find a way to correct the loss, even though it cannot.

## The Question of "Why"

Alongside "what if" comes another painful question: why.

Why this person?
Why now?
Why our family?
Why couldn't this have been prevented?

These questions often reach beyond personal responsibility and enter spiritual or existential territory. Some survivors struggle with anger toward fate, God, or the randomness of life itself.

The search for meaning is part of the human response to tragedy. Yet sometimes meaning cannot be fully understood.

Over time, many grieving siblings discover that healing does not come from answering every question, but from learning to live alongside the uncertainty.

# The Role of Regret

Regret is another powerful emotion that surfaces after the loss of a sibling.

People may regret:

- words spoken in anger
- time not spent together
- opportunities missed
- conversations never finished
- apologies never given

These regrets can feel heavy, especially when the chance to repair the relationship is gone.

However, it is important to remember that no relationship is perfect. Every sibling bond contains moments of closeness and moments of conflict. This is part of being human.

Regret does not erase the love that existed between siblings.

# Releasing the Burden of Perfect Responsibility

One of the most important steps in healing from sibling loss is recognizing the limits of personal responsibility.

No one person controls the course of another person's life. Even the most attentive sibling cannot predict every event or prevent every tragedy.

Grieving siblings often hold themselves to impossible standards of protection and foresight. Over time, learning to release these expectations can ease the burden of guilt.

Compassion toward oneself becomes essential.

## Transforming Questions into Reflection

Although the questions of "what if" and "why" may never disappear entirely, they can gradually shift in meaning.

Instead of becoming sources of punishment, they can become opportunities for reflection.

Some survivors eventually find themselves asking different questions:

What did my sibling teach me about life?
 How can I carry their memory forward?
 What kind of person do I want to become because of this experience?

These questions move the focus from blame toward meaning and growth.

## Living With Unanswered Questions

Grief does not always provide neat conclusions. Some questions remain unanswered forever.

Learning to live with uncertainty is one of the most difficult parts of the healing process. It requires patience, compassion, and the willingness to accept that some parts of life remain beyond human understanding.

Over time, many siblings discover that the intensity of the questions softens. They may still wonder about the past, but the thoughts no longer dominate every moment.

The love for the sibling remains, even as the search for answers slowly quiets.

## Conclusion of Chapter 7

The questions of "what if" and "why" are natural companions in the journey of grief. They arise from love, longing, and the human desire to make sense of tragedy.

Yet carrying these questions as accusations against oneself can deepen suffering. Healing often begins when survivors recognize that responsibility does not belong entirely to them.

By approaching these questions with compassion rather than blame, grieving siblings can begin to release the weight they have been carrying.

The past cannot be changed, but the future can still hold meaning, connection, and the enduring presence of love.

# Chapter 8:

*Rebuilding Identity After Loss*

When a sibling dies, the loss does not only remove a person from your life—it alters how you see yourself. Siblings are woven into our sense of identity. They witness our earliest memories, share our family history, and help shape the roles we play within the family and the world.

Because of this deep connection, losing a sibling can create an unexpected identity crisis. Survivors may find themselves asking questions they have never asked before: Who am I now? How do I move forward without the person who knew me best? What does my life look like without them in it?

This chapter explores how sibling loss reshapes identity and how survivors can gradually rebuild a sense of self while carrying their sibling's memory forward.

## The Role Siblings Play in Identity

From childhood onward, siblings help define who we are. They influence our personality, our confidence, and the way we relate to others.

A sibling may be:

• a protector

• a role model

• a rival

• a confidant

• a teammate in navigating family life

These relationships form the backdrop of our development. Even when siblings grow apart in adulthood, their influence remains embedded in memory and personality.

When that presence disappears, survivors may feel as though part of their personal story has been erased.

## Losing the Witness to Your Life

One of the most profound aspects of sibling loss is losing the person who witnessed your life from the beginning.

Siblings remember the details that others do not:

• childhood homes

• family traditions

• shared struggles

• inside jokes

• moments of growth and change

They hold pieces of your story that no one else carries in exactly the same way.

When a sibling dies, survivors may feel that a part of their history has vanished. The person who shared those memories is no longer there to confirm them, laugh about them, or understand them without explanation.

This loss can create a deep sense of disorientation.

## Changes in Family Roles

After a sibling's death, the roles within a family often shift. Birth order dynamics may change, and responsibilities that once belonged to the sibling who died may suddenly fall on someone else.

A middle child may become the oldest. A younger sibling may suddenly feel the weight of new expectations. The surviving sibling may feel pressure to replace the emotional role that was once filled by the sibling who is gone.

These changes can feel unsettling. Survivors may struggle to understand where they fit in the family structure now.

Over time, families begin to adjust, but the process can take patience and open communication.

# The Feeling of Being "Different"

Many surviving siblings report feeling fundamentally different after the loss.

They may notice changes in their perspective on life. Priorities shift. Activities that once felt important may lose meaning, while relationships and emotional connections become more significant.

This transformation is not unusual. Profound loss often changes how people see the world and themselves.

While these changes can feel confusing at first, they can also lead to personal growth and deeper self-awareness.

# Rediscovering the Self

Rebuilding identity after loss does not mean forgetting the sibling who died. Instead, it involves learning how to carry their memory while continuing to live your own life.

This process may include:

• reflecting on personal values
• exploring new interests or goals
• reconnecting with supportive relationships
• allowing space for both grief and hope

Identity reconstruction happens gradually. There is no fixed timeline for when someone should feel "like themselves again."

The person you become after loss may not be the same person you were before—but that does not mean the future cannot still hold meaning and fulfillment.

## Integrating the Sibling's Legacy

Many survivors find comfort in carrying aspects of their sibling's legacy forward.

This might include:

• living by values the sibling embodied
• continuing traditions they loved
• supporting causes that mattered to them
• sharing stories about them with others

Through these actions, the sibling's influence continues to shape the survivor's life.

Rather than disappearing, the bond evolves into a lasting presence that guides and inspires.

# Allowing Identity to Evolve

Grief does not freeze identity in time. Just as people grow and change throughout life, identity continues to evolve after loss.

Some survivors discover new strengths they did not know they possessed. Others find deeper empathy for the suffering of others. Many develop a renewed appreciation for life and relationships.

These changes do not erase the pain of losing a sibling. Instead, they become part of the story of how survivors adapt and continue forward.

# Conclusion of Chapter 8

Rebuilding identity after the loss of a sibling is a gradual and deeply personal journey. The absence of someone who helped shape your life can leave you feeling uncertain about who you are and where you belong.

Yet identity is not fixed. It continues to grow and evolve over time.

By honoring the bond you shared with your sibling while allowing yourself to move forward, it is possible to build a life that holds both grief and meaning. The relationship does not end with death—it transforms into memory, influence, and enduring love.

# Chapter 9:

*The Long Road of Healing*

Healing after the loss of a sibling is not a quick or predictable process. It unfolds slowly, often in ways that are difficult to recognize while they are happening. Many survivors expect grief to move in a straight line—from shock, to sadness, to eventual peace. In reality, grief rarely follows such a simple path.

Instead, healing often feels like a long road with unexpected turns. Some days bring moments of calm or acceptance, while other days reopen the ache of loss as if it has just occurred. Understanding that this uneven process is normal can help surviving siblings approach healing with patience rather than frustration.

This chapter explores the gradual nature of healing and the ways individuals learn to live with grief while continuing to build meaningful lives.

# Grief Is Not Linear

One of the most important truths about healing is that grief does not move in a straight line. Emotions may shift from day to day or even hour to hour.

A person may feel steady one moment and suddenly be overwhelmed by sadness the next. Memories, music, places, or unexpected reminders can bring grief back with surprising intensity.

These fluctuations do not mean healing is failing. They are part of the natural rhythm of grieving.

Over time, many survivors notice that the waves of grief still arrive, but they become less overwhelming and more manageable.

# The Early Stages of Adjustment

In the months following a sibling's death, daily life may feel unfamiliar. Routines that once felt normal can suddenly feel strange or empty.

Survivors may struggle with concentration, motivation, or emotional balance. Activities that once brought joy may feel distant or unimportant.

These experiences are common in early grief. The mind and body are adjusting to a reality that feels fundamentally changed.

Allowing time for this adjustment is an essential part of healing.

# Finding Support

Healing rarely happens in complete isolation. Support from others can play an important role in helping siblings navigate grief.

Support may come from:

- family members
- close friends
- grief support groups
- counselors or therapists
- spiritual or religious communities

Talking about the sibling who died, sharing memories, or simply expressing emotions can reduce the sense of isolation that often accompanies loss.

For some people, professional guidance provides a safe space to process complicated emotions such as guilt, anger, or confusion.

# The Role of Self-Compassion

Grieving siblings sometimes judge themselves harshly. They may feel they should be stronger, recover more quickly, or avoid emotional moments.

Practicing self-compassion can soften this pressure.

Self-compassion involves:

- recognizing that grief is a natural human response
- allowing emotions to surface without judgment
- understanding that healing takes time
- treating oneself with the same kindness offered to others

By approaching grief with patience and care, survivors create space for healing to unfold naturally.

# Moments of Unexpected Peace

As time passes, survivors often begin to notice small moments when the intensity of grief loosens.

These moments may appear unexpectedly—during a conversation with a friend, while enjoying a quiet evening, or while remembering a joyful memory of the sibling.

At first, these moments can feel surprising or even unsettling. Some survivors worry that feeling peace means they are forgetting the person they lost.

In reality, these moments often signal that the heart is learning to carry both grief and life at the same time.

# Continuing Bonds

One of the most powerful discoveries many siblings make during healing is that the relationship with the person who died does not completely disappear.

Instead, the bond changes form.

Survivors may continue to feel connected to their sibling through memories, shared traditions, personal values, or internal conversations.

They may sense their sibling's influence in important decisions, family gatherings, or personal milestones.

This concept, often called "continuing bonds," allows survivors to maintain a sense of connection while still moving forward with their lives.

# Growth Through Grief

Although grief is painful, some survivors eventually notice personal growth emerging from the experience.

They may develop deeper empathy for others who are suffering. They may strengthen relationships with family and friends. They may become more aware of the importance of time, love, and presence.

This growth does not mean the loss was beneficial or desired. Rather, it reflects the human capacity to adapt and find meaning even after profound hardship.

## Accepting the New Reality

Healing does not mean returning to the life that existed before the sibling died. That life has changed.

Instead, healing involves learning how to live within a new reality—one that includes both the memory of the sibling and the continuation of life.

Over time, the pain of loss may soften enough for survivors to engage fully with their lives again. They may pursue goals, build relationships, and create new experiences.

The love for the sibling remains, even as life continues to unfold.

## Conclusion of Chapter 9

The journey of healing after sibling loss is long and deeply personal. It unfolds in small steps, often unnoticed in the moment.

Grief does not disappear, but it gradually becomes woven into the fabric of life rather than dominating every thought and emotion.

Through patience, support, and compassion for oneself, surviving siblings can learn to carry both the memory of their loved one and the possibilities of the future.

Healing does not erase the bond. It allows that bond to live on in a different form.

---

# Chapter 10:

*Keeping Their Love Alive*

When a sibling dies, the relationship does not simply disappear. The physical presence may be gone, but the love, memories, and influence of that sibling continue to exist within the lives of those who remain.

One of the most meaningful parts of the healing journey involves finding ways to keep that love alive. Rather than trying to forget or move past the sibling who died, many survivors discover that honoring the relationship helps them move forward with greater peace.

This chapter explores the ways siblings can maintain a continuing connection with the person they lost while embracing the life that still lies ahead.

## Remembering Through Story

Stories play a powerful role in preserving the memory of someone who has died. Sharing memories allows the sibling's personality, humor, and experiences to remain part of everyday life.

Families often tell stories about:

- childhood adventures
- shared holidays
- funny misunderstandings
- personal achievements
- moments of kindness or courage

Each story keeps the sibling's presence alive in conversation and memory.

For surviving siblings, telling these stories can be both comforting and healing. It reinforces the idea that the person who died continues to matter.

## Honoring Traditions

Many families choose to honor the memory of a sibling by continuing traditions that were important to them.

This might include:

- preparing a favorite meal on special occasions
- playing music they loved
- visiting places that held meaning
- celebrating their birthday with family gatherings
- participating in activities they enjoyed

These traditions transform remembrance into an active expression of love.

Rather than focusing only on the loss, they allow families to celebrate the life that was lived.

# Creating Personal Rituals

Some surviving siblings develop personal rituals that help them feel connected to the person they lost.

These rituals might be simple and private, such as:

• lighting a candle on significant dates
• writing letters to the sibling
• keeping a journal of memories
• visiting meaningful locations
• spending quiet time reflecting on shared experiences

Rituals provide structure for grief and create moments where remembrance is intentional rather than accidental.

# Carrying Their Values Forward

A sibling's influence often extends far beyond their lifetime. The lessons they shared, the values they lived by, and the love they offered continue shaping the lives of those who knew them.

Surviving siblings sometimes honor that influence by:

• practicing the kindness their sibling showed others
• supporting causes that mattered to them
• living with the courage or humor the sibling embodied
• sharing the sibling's story with younger generations

Through these actions, the sibling's spirit continues to affect the world.

## Finding Meaning in Legacy

Legacy does not have to involve large public gestures. Often, it appears in small everyday choices.

A surviving sibling might become more attentive to family relationships. They may value time with loved ones more deeply. They may approach life with a renewed appreciation for connection and compassion.

These changes form part of the sibling's legacy—a quiet continuation of the love that existed between them.

## Allowing Joy to Return

One of the most difficult parts of healing can be allowing joy to return without feeling guilty.

Many survivors struggle with the idea that happiness might somehow diminish the importance of the sibling who died.

In truth, joy and remembrance can coexist. The ability to experience happiness again does not erase grief or love. Instead, it reflects the resilience of the human heart.

Over time, survivors may find that joyful moments often include memories of the sibling who is no longer physically present.

## The Enduring Bond

The relationship between siblings does not end with death. It changes form, but the emotional connection can remain strong.

Many survivors report continuing to feel their sibling's presence in subtle ways—through memories, dreams, or moments that remind them of shared experiences.

Others feel the connection through the influence their sibling had on their character, values, and outlook on life.

This enduring bond becomes part of the survivor's identity and continues shaping their life in meaningful ways.

## Living Forward With Love

The goal of healing is not to leave the sibling behind. Instead, it is to carry their love into the future.

Surviving siblings learn to build lives that include both remembrance and new experiences. They continue forming relationships, pursuing goals, and creating memories while still honoring the bond they shared.

Life after loss is different, but it can still hold beauty, connection, and purpose.

## Conclusion of Chapter 10

Keeping a sibling's love alive is not about clinging to the past. It is about allowing the relationship to evolve in a new form.

Through memories, traditions, personal rituals, and everyday acts of kindness, the influence of the sibling who died continues to shape the lives of those who loved them.

Grief may never disappear entirely, but love does not disappear either.

In time, many surviving siblings discover that the bond they shared becomes a guiding presence—one that encourages them to live with greater compassion, gratitude, and courage.

The journey that began with loss ultimately becomes a journey of remembrance, growth, and enduring love.

# The Weaver of the Light

When the silence dropped, the first shard fell, And broke the mirror where two lives would dwell. The loss arrived, profound, yet strangely veiled, A bond uncounted, suddenly curtailed. We stand dismembered, searching for the face that held our history, our time, our place. We wrestle ghosts of if only and of blame, While fragile family whispers out your name.

The shattered self asks: Who am I alone? A path uncharted, a familiar road unshown. We ride the wild grief, where the mood swings climb, Unmasking anger lost outside of time.

The weight of things: the empty, folded clothes, The anniversaries the memory knows. The heavy backpack, truth we learn to bear, A constant pressure, a specific, aching care. But in the dark, the hand finds tools to cling, A conscious breath, the solace comfort brings.

We learn to pause, to count the senses five, To  anchor gently, proving we survive. For courage waits not in the absence of the dread, But in the small steps, consciously ahead. We seek not closure, which the world proclaims,

But integration, whisper-soft as flames. And here, the turn: the painful truth we find— That love's persistence leaves a light behind. We shift the mourning to active purpose sought, A legacy embodied, bought with dearly thought.

We take your value, humor, strength, and grace, And give it breathing room within this space. So, we move forward, not away, but through, Our life a vessel carrying the love of you.

The pain still echoes, but the volume yields, To open spaces, and to sunlit fields. We weave the fabric, broken, whole, and vast,

A new horizon built on what has passed.

# About the Author

Lin Law is a writer, speaker, and advocate dedicated to shedding light on the complexities of sibling loss—a grief often overlooked but deeply profound. Her journey to write *Moving Forward from Grief* was born directly out of her own devastating experience of losing her very own siblings to complications from lupus and sudden death in 2022 and 2024.

For years, Lin Law struggled to find resources that truly acknowledged the unique devastation of losing a brother or sister. Her professional background in counseling, combined with her personal lived experience, provided her with the unique perspective necessary to create this comprehensive guide—one that is both deeply empathetic and structurally practical.

Lin Law currently lives in the state of Alabama. When she is not writing or facilitating grief support workshops, women's conferences, etc., she can be found traveling internationally, assisting youth and families with spiritual elevation and building.

Through her writing, Lin Law hopes to ensure that no surviving sibling feels invisible in their pain, providing the permission and the tools they need to integrate their loss and find a new horizon of hope.

You can connect with Lin Law and learn more about her work through her social media handles provided, and also by email at lindalaw08@icloud.com.